THE REALLY USEFUL LITTLE BOOK OF KNOTS

For Doris at Cottage Farm

THE REALLY USEFUL
— LITTLE —
BOOK OF KNOTS

PETER OWEN

Design and illustrations by Peter Owen

Printed in the United States of America.

10 9 8 7 6 5 4

Library of Congress Cataloging-in-Publication Data

Owen, Peter, 1950-
    The really useful little book of knots / Peter Owen.
        p. cm.
    ISBN 1-58080-124-2 (pbk.)
    1. Knots and splices--Handbooks, manuals, etc. I. Title.

VM533.O94325 2004
623.88'82--dc22   2004012947

CONTENTS

INTRODUCTION

In an ever-changing world that can supply a gadget to solve almost every conceivable problem, it is rare and comforting to come across a simple, practical, problem-solving activity that is still as useful now as it has been in generations past. Tying a knot is a simple and practical solution that can solve many everyday problems.

The Really Useful Little Book of Knots will show you how to tie and use 20 of the most useful and practical knots for everyday use at work, home, or play. This book does not pretend to be a knot encyclopedia; nor is it aimed at outdoor pursuit specialists like mountaineers or sailors. It contains no knot-tying jargon or technical terms, just easy-to-follow, clear step-by-step instructions for a handful of very useful and practical knots that will cope with most jobs and situations that the average person will encounter.

Not knowing how to correctly tie and use a knot is not only very frustrating but can also spell disaster in even the simplest of situations. By helping you choose the right knot for the job and tie it correctly, this incredibly handy little book will help you eliminate those potential disasters and make life run just a little smoother.

KNOT-TYING MATERIAL

It is possible to tie a knot with an extremely wide variety of materials both human-made and natural. But the most commonly used materials are rope, cord, string, and twine. Rope is traditionally anything over 0.5inch or 12mm in diameter. Ropes are also often referred to as lines. Smaller stuff, as it is informally called, is cordage; strings and twines are generally even thinner.

All of these materials used to be made by twisting natural fibers together. Natural fibers such as manila, sisal, coir, hemp, flax, and cotton were first twisted into yarn, then into strands, and finally into rope of all different sizes.

Artificial or synthetic materials have now almost completely replaced natural fibers. These human-made materials can be manufactured to run the whole length of a line and do not vary in thickness; this gives them superior strength.

Nylon, first produced in 1938 for domestic use, was the first human-made material to be used in this way. Since then wide ranges of artificial rope, cord, string, and twine have been developed to meet different purposes. Size for size they are lighter, stronger, and cheaper than their natural counterparts. They do not rot or mildew; they are resistant to sunlight, chemicals, oil, gasoline, and most common solvents. They can also be manufactured in a wide range of colors and patterns. Color-coded ropes make for instant recognition of lines of different function and size.

Artificial rope, cord, string, and twine do have some disadvantages, the main one being that they melt when heated. Even the friction generated when one rope rubs against another may be enough to cause damage, so if you use artificial ropes in this situation it is vital to check them regularly. Another disadvantage is that artificial ropes are generally very smooth, unlike the older natural-fiber ropes, and this can lead to knots slipping and coming undone. In this situation additional stopper or security knots may be required.

Rope is sturdy material, but it is expensive, so it's worth looking after it properly. Always coil rope carefully when not in use and make sure it is stored in dry conditions.

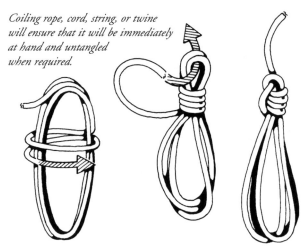

Coiling rope, cord, string, or twine will ensure that it will be immediately at hand and untangled when required.

TYPES OF ROPE

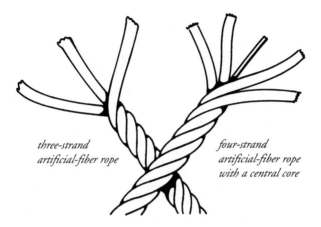

*three-strand
artificial-fiber rope*

*four-strand
artificial-fiber rope
with a central core*

Twisted or Laid Rope

Artificial rope can be twisted or laid like old-style natural-fiber rope. Usually three strands of nylon filaments are twisted together to form a length of rope, cord, string, or twine. There are variations on this available. One very strong variation is four strands of nylon filament twisted around a central nylon core.

The cost of twisted or laid rope is generally about two-thirds that of the more widely used braided rope; see page 10. Twisted or laid rope, made of thick multifilaments tightly twisted together, may be very resistant to wear, but it may also be difficult to handle because of its stiffness. As a general rule, do not buy rope that is too stiff.

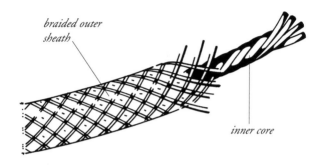

braided outer sheath

inner core

Braided Rope

The combination of an outer sheath surrounding an inner core makes braided rope softer, more flexible, and generally a lot stronger than other types of synthetic rope.

The outer sheath generally consists of 16 strands. This surrounds an inner core that can be parallel fibers, or twisted, or plaited. Both the sheath and the core contribute the strength and flexibility of the rope. Its flexibility makes it ideal for knot tying, and the smoothness of the outer sheath makes the rope easy and comfortable to handle.

It is very often thought that braided rope is only manufactured in larger-diameter sizes, but modern technology also enables this highly successful material to be manufactured in very small-diameter sizes.

HOW TO USE THIS BOOK

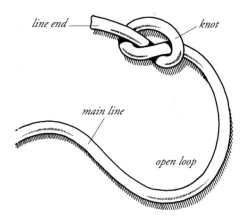

line end — *knot*

main line

open loop

This book makes a conscious effort to avoid any knot-tying jargon or technical terms—for example, the end of a line is simply called a line end.

The diagrams accompanying the tying instructions are intended to be self-explanatory, but additional written instructions are included at specific points in the tying procedure. There are arrows to show the direction in which you should push or pull, and dotted lines indicate intermediate positions. In many of the illustrations, lines are shown faded out or cut short for clarity. When tying a knot, you should always have sufficient working line end to complete the knot. This can often be calculated by looking at the illustration of the finished knot.

OVERHAND KNOT

This is the best-known and most widely used of all knots; it is the knot that we can all tie. It does form the basis for many other knots and is often tied in conjunction with other knots. The most common use for this knot is as a stopper knot at the end of a piece of string, cord, or rope—for example, at the end of a length of sewing thread to stop the thread from passing through the eye of a needle.

SUGGESTED USES

- A stopper knot to prevent the end of a piece of string or cord from fraying.
- A stopper knot to prevent the end of a line from passing through an eye, loop, or hole.
- Tied at regular intervals along a line, it can make the line easier to grip.
- Tied in conjunction with other knots, it can be used as an additional safety measure to prevent slippage.

> |

TYING INSTRUCTIONS

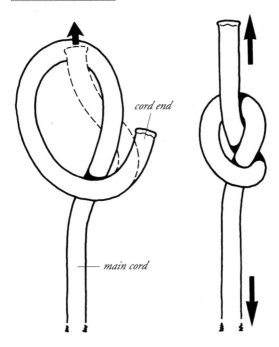

cord end

main cord

1 *Double the cord to form a loop and then bring the cord end over the main cord and under the loop. Then pull out through the loop in the direction of the arrow.*

2 *Position the knot where it is required in the cord and then tighten the completed knot by pulling in the direction of the arrows.*

continued next page >

> *Overhand Knot continued*

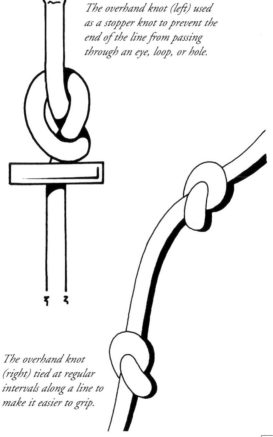

The overhand knot (left) used as a stopper knot to prevent the end of the line from passing through an eye, loop, or hole.

The overhand knot (right) tied at regular intervals along a line to make it easier to grip.

>

A SIMPLE NOOSE FORMED WITH AN OVERHAND KNOT

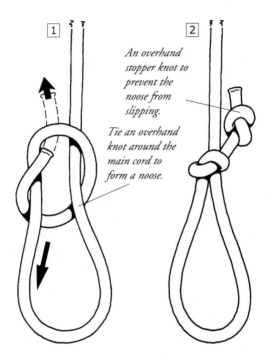

An overhand stopper knot to prevent the noose from slipping.

Tie an overhand knot around the main cord to form a noose.

A simple noose can be quickly formed using an overhand knot. The noose can be tied first, placed over an object, and then tightened, or can be given its simple construction tied directly around an object. This type of noose is often the best way to start tying a parcel or to get an initial grip on an object. A second overhand knot can be added to the end of the line to prevent the noose from slipping.

MULTIPLE OVERHAND KNOT

This is a quick and easy way to tie a decorative stopper knot that is often used at the end of cords to prevent fraying or to stop the cord from pulling out of holes or openings. It can also add weight to the end of a cord and is still used today by nuns and monks to embellish the end of the cord tied around their waists and to make the cord hang properly. The appearance and size of the knot can be varied with the number of turns used to tie it.

SUGGESTED USES

- A decorative stopper knot to prevent the end of a piece of string or cord from fraying.
- A decorative stopper knot to prevent the end of a line from passing through an eye, loop, or hole.
- To weight the end of a line to make it hang properly—for example, a light switch cord.
- A decorative separator for beads threaded on a string—for example, a bracelet or necklace.

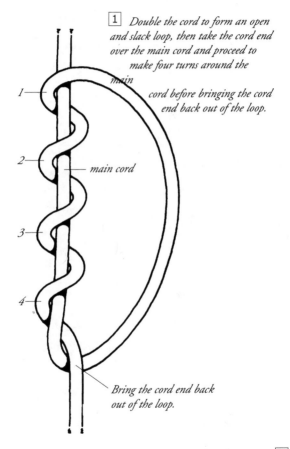

1 *Double the cord to form an open and slack loop, then take the cord end over the main cord and proceed to make four turns around the main*

cord before bringing the cord end back out of the loop.

1

2 — main cord

3

4

Bring the cord end back out of the loop.

continued next page >

> *Multiple Overhand Knot continued*

2 *(left) Slowly and evenly pull on the two cord ends, allowing the two ends to twist in opposite directions; the knot will start to form.*

3 *(below) Tighten the final knot as you work the knot into its final even-looking form with your fingers—a bit like forming plasticine. If the knot is to be positioned at the end of a cord, trim the cord end accordingly.*

>

MULTIPLE OVERHAND KNOT VARIATIONS

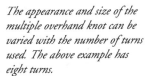

The appearance and size of the multiple overhand knot can be varied with the number of turns used. The above example has eight turns.

The decorative appearance of the multiple overhand knot is often used as a feature—for example, as above, a bead separator in

REEF KNOT

The reef knot, or square knot, is one of the most
commonly known knots and often is the only knot
many people know apart from the granny knot;
see page 23. It is used to join together the
ends of the same rope or string and should
only be used as a temporary join in lines
of identical type, weight, and diameter.
The reef knot is not a secure knot
and should not be used as one.
Using it as a binding knot where
it can press against whatever it
is securing will ensure that the
more strain is placed on it,
the tighter it is pulled.

see page 23.

SUGGESTED USES

- A quick and easy, temporary (unsecure) join for the two
  ends of the same piece of rope or string.
- A quick and easy, temporary (unsecure) join for two
  lines of identical type, weight, and diameter.
- As a binding knot, ideal for bandages and slings.

TYING INSTRUCTIONS

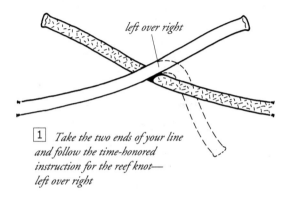

left over right

1 *Take the two ends of your line and follow the time-honored instruction for the reef knot— left over right*

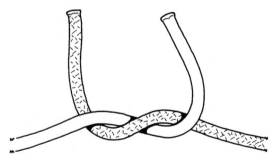

2 *Twist the left line under the right line to form the above, leaving enough line for the second part of the knot.*

continued next page >

> *Reef Knot continued*

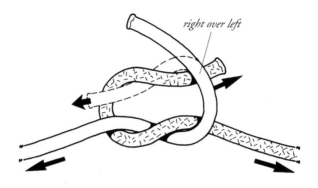

right over left

3 *Take the two remaining ends and—right over left. Start to form the knot by pulling slowly and evenly on the two line ends and the two main line sections.*

4 *Tighten the final knot into its even and balanced form as above. If the knot is raised and uneven, you have tied a granny knot; see the following page.*

>

REEF KNOT VARIATIONS

The reef knot is an ideal knot for tying pieces of material together and is especially suited to bandages and slings.

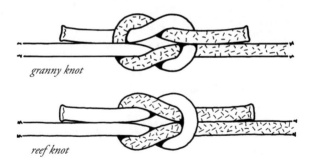

granny knot

reef knot

When tying the reef knot, be careful to avoid the unreliable granny knot. Remember the simple tying instruction, "Left over right, then right over left."

FIGURE-EIGHT LOOP

This is one of the best-known and most widely used
of all knots. It is probably the safest and
quickest way to form a strong loop or
eye at the end of a rope. It is easy to
tie and will not slip or work loose.
As a testament to this knot's
strength and usefulness, it is the
favored loop knot used by
climbers and mountaineers
to attach ropes to various
pieces of climbing
equipment.

SUGGESTED USES

- A loop to hold in your hand to pull or hold on to
  an object.
- Interlink two loops to quickly join and unjoin two
  ropes; see page 27.
- A loop to place over or around an object.
- A loop to clip or hang on to an object.

>

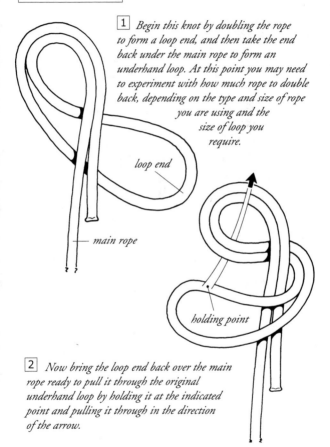

1 *Begin this knot by doubling the rope to form a loop end, and then take the end back under the main rope to form an underhand loop. At this point you may need to experiment with how much rope to double back, depending on the type and size of rope you are using and the size of loop you require.*

loop end

main rope

holding point

2 *Now bring the loop end back over the main rope ready to pull it through the original underhand loop by holding it at the indicated point and pulling it through in the direction of the arrow.*

continued next page >

> *Figure-Eight Loop continued*

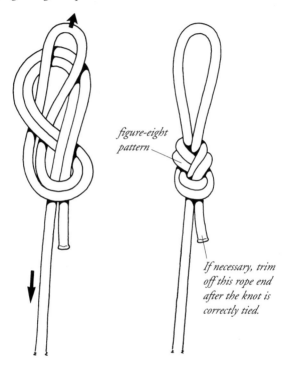

figure-eight
pattern

If necessary, trim
off this rope end
after the knot is
correctly tied.

3 Pull the doubled loop end
through the original
underhand loop and slowly
draw the knot together by
pulling the loop end and the

4 Finally, tighten the
completed knot, making sure
that the figure-eight pattern
and the loop have been
correctly formed.

>

INTERLOCKED FIGURE-EIGHT LOOP KNOT

Two figure-eight loop knots can be interlinked to create a quick and easy method of securely joining two ropes. Interlink the loops (fig. 1) and tighten by pulling on the two main ropes. The final interlinked knot (fig. 2) can then be easily broken by pushing the two figure-eight loops together to loosen the joint and then unlinking the two loops.

SHEET BEND

The sheet bend is a good general-purpose utility knot for joining two lines together or to attach a line to anything that has an opening to pass the line through to enable the line to be trapped under itself. The sheet bend is a quick and easy knot to tie, can withstand great strains, and is easily undone afterward. Unlike most other line-joining knots, the sheet bend can be used for joining two lines of different diameter and material—but caution does need to be exercised here that the two lines are not too dissimilar.

SUGGESTED USES

- To join two lines togther of different diameter and material.
- To attach to any object with an opening that will enable the line to pass through and be trapped under itself; see page 31.
- In a situation where the knot will be under great strain—the greater the strain on a sheet bend, the better the jamming action.

TYING INSTRUCTIONS

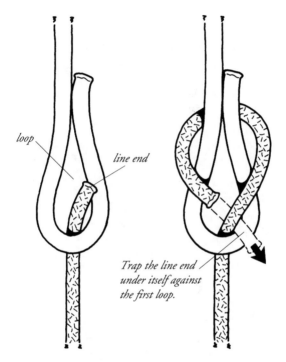

loop

line end

Trap the line end under itself against the first loop.

1 *Form a small loop with one of the lines to be joined. Pass the other line end up through the loop.*

2 *Take the line end around the back of the loop and then back under itself, trapping it against the original loop.*

continued next page >

> *Sheet Bend continued*

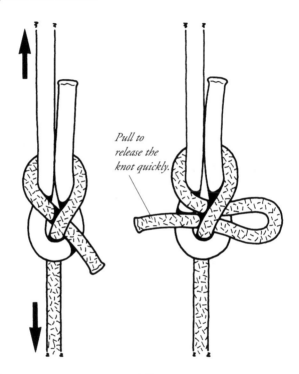

Pull to release the knot quickly.

3 *Tighten the final knot by evenly pulling on both lines. The strain will create the jamming action.*

4 *If a quick-release knot is required, double the jammed line back on itself to create a "slip" that can be pulled for quick release.*

>

ATTACHING A SHEET BEND TO AN OBJECT

A sheet bend can be adapted to fasten a line to anything that has an opening through which you can pass a single line that can be trapped under itself—for example,

attaching a line to a tool handle to be lifted, lowered, or hung. By using the "slipped" version of the sheet bend, you can quickly release the tool when required.

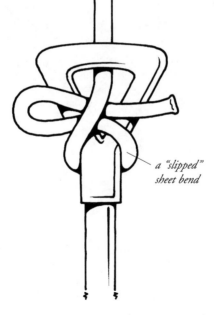

a "slipped" sheet bend

FISHERMAN'S KNOT

This simple knot is made up of two overhand knots
that jam against each other. It is a very strong
knot used for joining two similar lines of equal
diameter. It is most effective when used with
smaller-diameter material such as string, cord,
and twine and as its name suggests, very
effective with fishing line. It is not suitable
for use with large- or medium-diameter
rope. Normally this knot can be easily
untied by pulling apart the two
overhand knots and then untying
them separately. To make this
knot even stronger and more
robust, you can tie a variation
using a double overhand
knot at each end; see
page 35.

see
page 35.

SUGGESTED USES

- A strong knot for joining two similar lines of equal
  diameter.
- Especially suited to small-diameter material—for
  example, fishing line.

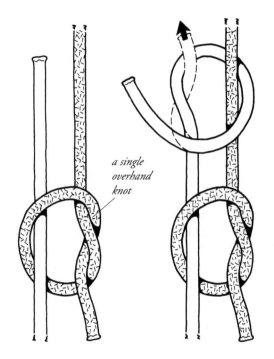

a single overhand knot

1 *Lay the ends of two cords parallel to each other and make a single overhand knot in one end around the other cord.*

2 *Repeat this operation with the end of the other cord to tie an identical single overhand knot around the first cord.*

continued next page

> Fisherman's Knot continued

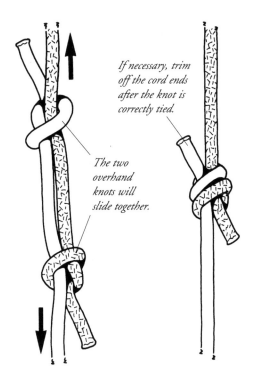

If necessary, trim off the cord ends after the knot is correctly tied.

The two overhand knots will slide together.

3 Tighten the two overhand knots and then pull the two main cord sections to slide the overhand knots together.

4 Continue pulling the knots until they snugly fit together and then pull hard to jam the knots to form the final knot.

DOUBLE FISHERMAN'S KNOT

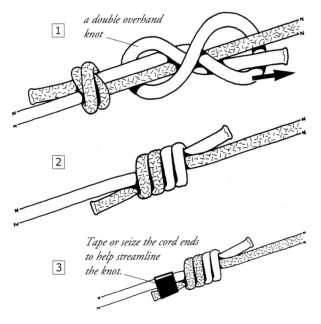

1 — *a double overhand knot*

2

3 — *Tape or seize the cord ends to help streamline the knot.*

To make the fisherman's knot even stronger and more robust, tie the double version. Simply replace a single overhand knot on each cord with a double overhand knot (fig. 1). Jam the two knots together to form the final knot (fig. 2). Depending on the type of material used to tie the knot, the double version can be quite bulky, so to streamline the knot tape or seize the cord ends (fig. 3); this will prevent the knot from catching on objects and minimize the risk of the overhand knot's working loose.

ROUND TURN & TWO HALF HITCHES

This knot is a true all-arounder: It is strong, dependable, and never jams. You can use it whenever you want to fasten a line to a ring, stake, post, pole, handle, or rail. Once the end of a rope has been secured with a round turn and two half hitches, the other end can be tied with a second knot. This is especially useful for fastening down unwieldy, bulky objects. Its name describes exactly what it is made up of, a round turn and two half hitches; for more information on hitches, see page 39.

for more information on hitches, see page 39.

SUGGESTED USES

- To quickly and securely attach a line to a ring, stake, post, pole, handle, or rail.
- To tie down or secure loads, especially unwieldy or bulky objects, to a car roof rack or trailer.
- To support loads of any description.
- To moor boats.

>

TYING INSTRUCTIONS

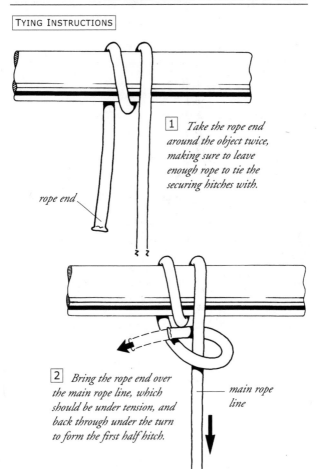

1 *Take the rope end around the object twice, making sure to leave enough rope to tie the securing hitches with.*

rope end

2 *Bring the rope end over the main rope line, which should be under tension, and back through under the turn to form the first half hitch.*

main rope line

continued next page >

> *Round Turn & Two Half Hitches continued*

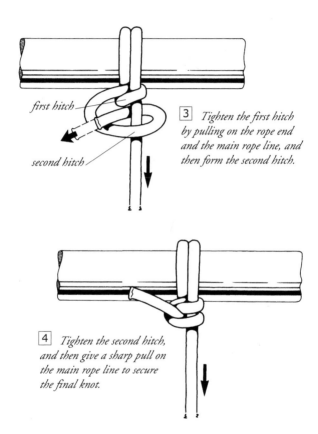

first hitch

second hitch

3 *Tighten the first hitch by pulling on the rope end and the main rope line, and then form the second hitch.*

4 *Tighten the second hitch, and then give a sharp pull on the main rope line to secure the final knot.*

>

HALF HITCHES

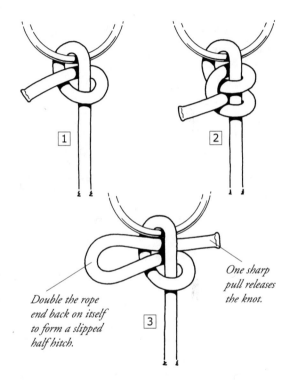

Double the rope end back on itself to form a slipped half hitch.

One sharp pull releases the knot.

The half hitch is a very widely used fastening. It can be used on its own in single form (fig. 1) or for extra strength in double form (fig. 2) or a very useful slipped form (fig. 3)—one sharp pull releases the knot. Alternatively, it can be used to complete and strengthen other knots, as in the round turn and two half hitches.

UNI-KNOT

The uni-knot, also known as the grinner knot, is a very secure and widely used fishing knot used for tying either an artificial fly or an eyed hook to fishing line or in its double form—the double uni-knot (see page 43)—for tying two pieces of fishing line together. It can also be used as a very secure general-purpose knot for joining a line to any object with an opening or for joining two lines together. Because it can be a bulky knot, depending on how many turns you use, it is more suited to thin line, cord, or rope and should only be used for joining lines of a similar type and diameter.

SUGGESTED USES

- For attaching an artificial fly or eyed fishing hook to fishing line.
- For securely joining two small-diameter lines together—for example, fishing line or small-diameter synthetic cord.
- For attaching to any small object with an opening or handle—for example, a key, whistle, or flashlight.

[>]

TYING INSTRUCTIONS

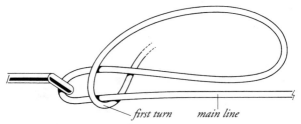

*sufficient line
to complete the knot*

1 *Thread the line through the object
opening, making sure to leave sufficient line
to complete the knot—this may have to be
established by trial and error.*

opening

first turn   main line

2 *Bring the threaded line back on itself to form
a loose loop, and then start to make the first turn
around the main line.*

continued next page >

> *Uni-Knot continued*

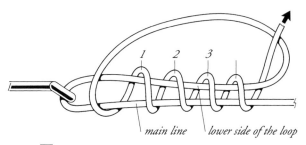

main line   *lower side of the loop*

3   Complete the first turn by taking the line back
through the loop, over the lower side of the loop, and
around the main line again. Make approximately
four turns and then bring the line end out through
the loop. Try to keep the knot as compact as possible
in the tying stage.

*If necessary, trim off
the line ends after the
knot is correctly tied.*

4   With the knot loosely formed, hold the object
and slowly pull on the main line. As the line tightens,
the final knot will form.

>

DOUBLE UNI-KNOT

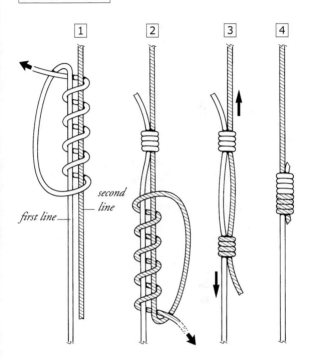

The double uni-knot is used to join two lines together. Lay the two lines side by side and tie a single uni-knot with the first line around the second line (fig. 1). Tighten the first uni-knot and then repeat the process with the second line (fig. 2). With both knots tightened, pull on both lines to start drawing the two knots together (fig. 3). Engage the two knots and then pull to tighten the final knot (fig. 4). If necessary, trim off the line ends after the knot is correctly tied.

BOWLINE

The bowline (say *boh-linn*) is used to form a fixed loop at the end of a line or to attach a line to an object. It is simple to tie, strong, and stable. The bowline's main advantages are that it does not slip, come loose, or jam. It is also quick and easy to untie, even when the line is under tension, by pushing the main line in the direction of the knot. It is a knot that can work loose if it is tied with stiff or slippery line, so to be really safe, finish the knot off with a stopper knot or extra half hitch.

SUGGESTED USES

- A fixed loop to hold in your hand to pull or hold on to an object.
- A fixed loop to tie around your waist, or someone else's waist, in a rescue situation.
- A fixed loop to place over or around an object—for example, when hoisting or dragging an object.

> ▶

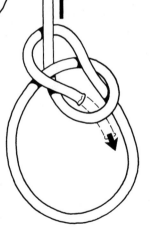

1 *First estimate the size of loop you require, and then at the point you want to position the knot, form a small loop in the main line. Bring the line end up and through the loop.*

main line

line end

knot position

2 *Take the line end around the back of the main line and back down into the small loop. Pull the line end through the loop, hold it in position, and then slowly start to pull the main line.*

continued next page >

> *Bowline continued*

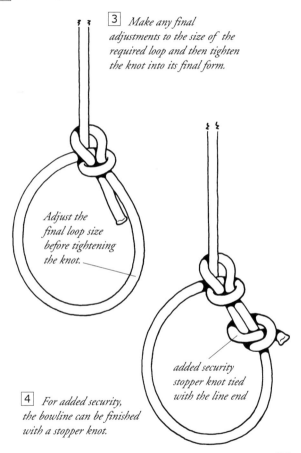

3 *Make any final adjustments to the size of the required loop and then tighten the knot into its final form.*

Adjust the final loop size before tightening the knot.

added security stopper knot tied with the line end

4 *For added security, the bowline can be finished with a stopper knot.*

>

THE RUNNING BOWLINE

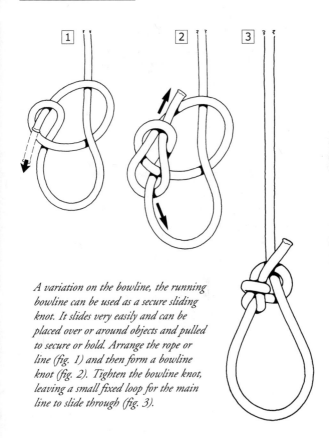

A variation on the bowline, the running bowline can be used as a secure sliding knot. It slides very easily and can be placed over or around objects and pulled to secure or hold. Arrange the rope or line (fig. 1) and then form a bowline knot (fig. 2). Tighten the bowline knot, leaving a small fixed loop for the main line to slide through (fig. 3).

CLOVE HITCH

The clove hitch is one of the more commonly known and useful of knots. It is used to fasten a line to a peg, pole, post, or ring, or to another rope that is not part of the knot. It is an easy knot to tie, and can with practice be tied with just one hand—useful when you're trying to hold the object you are tying up with the other hand. The clove hitch is not, however, a totally secure knot; it will work loose if the strain is intermittent and comes from different angles. Under these types of conditions it is best used as a temporary hold, and then replaced by a more stable knot.

SUGGESTED USES

- A quick and simple way to attach a line to a peg, post, pole, or ring—for example, securing tent guylines to pegs.
- A way of attaching one line to another line, as long as the required strain will remain steady and at right angles.

TYING INSTRUCTIONS

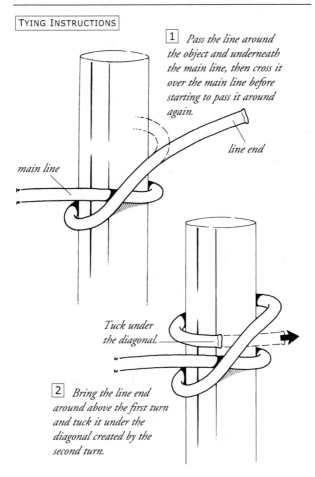

1 *Pass the line around the object and underneath the main line, then cross it over the main line before starting to pass it around again.*

line end

main line

Tuck under the diagonal.

2 *Bring the line end around above the first turn and tuck it under the diagonal created by the second turn.*

continued next page >

> *Clove Hitch continued*

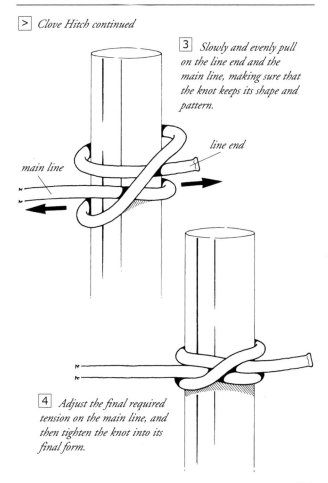

3 Slowly and evenly pull on the line end and the main line, making sure that the knot keeps its shape and pattern.

line end

main line

4 Adjust the final required tension on the main line, and then tighten the knot into its final form.

>

CLOVE HITCH—MADE ON A RING

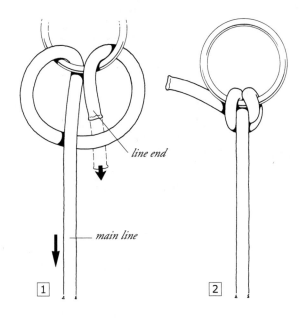

line end

main line

1

2

The clove hitch is just as quick and easy to tie on a ring as it is on a peg, post, or rail. Take the line end up through the ring, around the back of the main line, up through the ring again, and then down through the loop that has been created (fig. 1). Tighten the knot into its final form (fig. 2) by pulling on the main line. The clove hitch tied on a ring may visually appear different from one tied on a peg, post, or rail, but closer examination will show an identical form.

HIGHWAYMAN'S HITCH

The name of this knot allegedly comes from its use by highwaymen and bandits to give them quick release of their horses' reins and so ensure a fast getaway. The main part of the rope can be put under substantial tension, but one sharp pull on the rope end and the knot is undone. It is a knot for temporary fastenings and is especially useful when a quick release is required. It is a simple knot, both to make and to untie.

- Temporary tethering of animals.
- Mooring small boats.
- A temporary fastening that requires a quick release—for example, lowering a load.

>

TYING INSTRUCTIONS

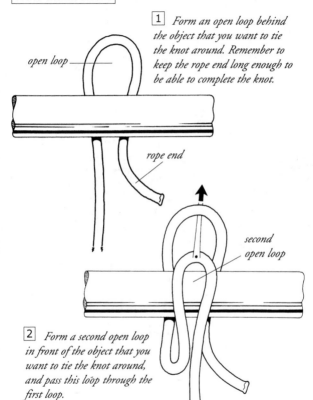

1 *Form an open loop behind the object that you want to tie the knot around. Remember to keep the rope end long enough to be able to complete the knot.*

open loop

rope end

second open loop

2 *Form a second open loop in front of the object that you want to tie the knot around, and pass this loop through the first loop.*

continued next page >

> *Highwayman's Hitch continued*

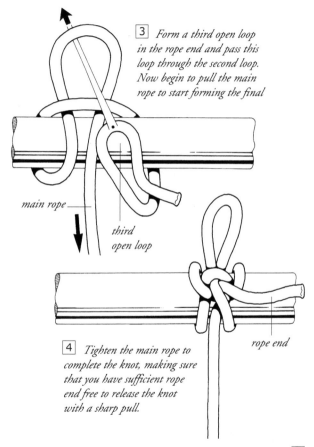

3 *Form a third open loop in the rope end and pass this loop through the second loop. Now begin to pull the main rope to start forming the final*

main rope

third open loop

4 *Tighten the main rope to complete the knot, making sure that you have sufficient rope end free to release the knot with a sharp pull.*

rope end

>

HIGHWAYMAN'S HITCH QUICK RELEASE

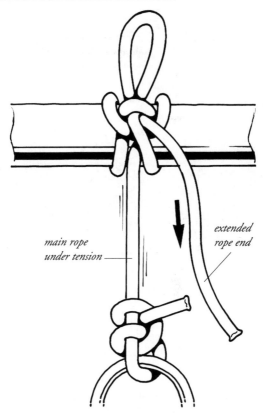

main rope
under tension

extended
rope end

The addition of a long rope end will give the option of releasing the knot from a distance. One sharp pull and the knot is released.

WAGGONER'S HITCH

This very useful, practical, and simple knot makes it possible to pull tight a line or rope and secure it, yet leave it ready for immediate release. This makes it an ideal knot for securing objects or loads. Once the line has been pulled tight, it should be secured with at least two half hitches.

SUGGESTED USES

- For securing a load to a wagon or truck.
- For securing several objects together.
- For applying tension to a line or rope that is used to hold an object or group of objects down.
- For securing an object or load that will require a quick and easy release.

> |

TYING INSTRUCTIONS

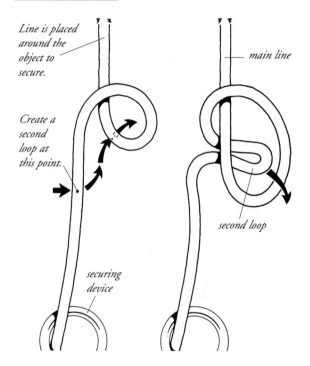

Line is placed around the object to secure.

Create a second loop at this point.

securing device

main line

second loop

1 *Place the line around the object to secure and then through or around the securing device. Twist an overhand loop into the main part of the line, and then create a second loop.*

2 *Pinch the second loop together, and then pass it through the first loop from underneath the main line.*

continued next page

> *Waggoner's Hitch continued*

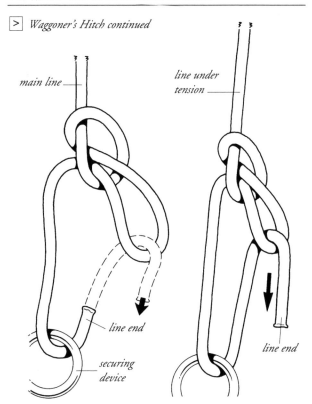

main line

line under tension

line end

securing device

line end

3 Pass the line end through the resulting second loop and pull in the opposite direction to the main line.

4 The required tension can now be applied by pulling the line end. Once the line is tightened, secure the line end.

A SECURED WAGGONER'S HITCH

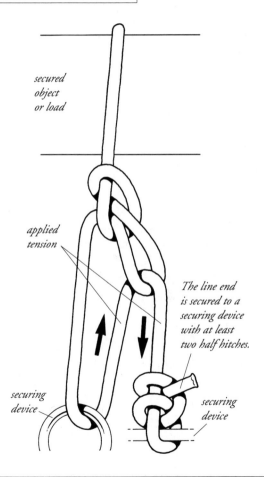

secured object or load

applied tension

The line end is secured to a securing device with at least two half hitches.

securing device

securing device

CONSTRICTOR KNOT

This is one of the best binding knots—it is a popular all-purpose knot that will grip tightly and stay tied. In fact, often the only way to release this knot is to cut it free. The constrictor knot can be used in any situation where you want to clamp or reinforce an object—for example, to clamp hose-pipe joints together or to hold two glued objects together while they dry. It is a knot that is used specifically for permanent fastenings, but you can effectively use it as a secure temporary fastening by introducing a slip knot into the final tuck, allowing you to release the knot with a sharp pull.

SUGGESTED USES

- To clamp two objects together—for example, hose-pipe joints.
- To securely close the neck of sacks and bags—for example, a garbage sack.
- To reinforce a structure—for example, garden plant supports that have been weakened or collapsed.

>

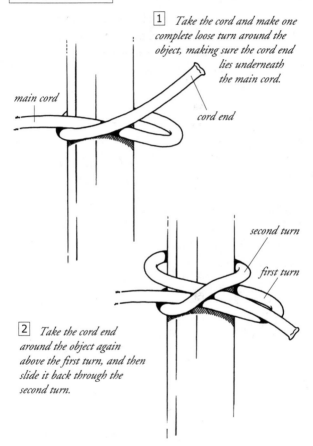

1 *Take the cord and make one complete loose turn around the object, making sure the cord end lies underneath the main cord.*

main cord

cord end

second turn

first turn

2 *Take the cord end around the object again above the first turn, and then slide it back through the second turn.*

continued next page >>

> *Constrictor Knot continued*

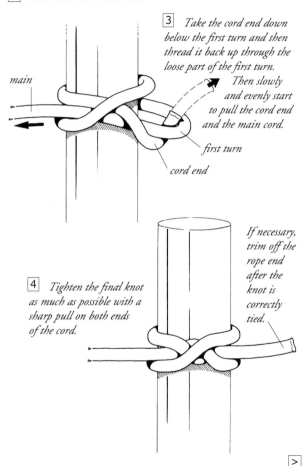

3 *Take the cord end down below the first turn and then thread it back up through the loose part of the first turn.*

Then slowly and evenly start to pull the cord end and the main cord.

main

first turn

cord end

If necessary, trim off the rope end after the knot is correctly tied.

4 *Tighten the final knot as much as possible with a sharp pull on both ends of the cord.*

>

CONSTRICTOR KNOT USES

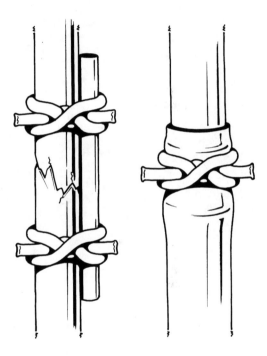

Constrictor knots are excellent for reinforcing broken or rotten structures.

The strong clamping properties of a constrictor knot can be used to create a secure hose-pipe joint.

TRANSOM KNOT

This is an excellent knot for fixing together cross-pieces of wood, bamboo, etc., and is often used in the garden for trellis work or supports for plants. Tied correctly, it is a knot that will not slip and so is especially useful for securely fixing objects—for example, skis or bikes to luggage racks. It is also widely used in the outdoors for building shelters or temporary structures. Once tied, the knot ends can be trimmed off for neatness. Although it can be prised undone, it is often simpler to just cut it through the diagonal.

SUGGESTED USES

- For fixing together cross-pieces of wood, bamboo, etc.
- For securely fixing objects to another object—for example, skis or bikes to a luggage rack.
- As a way of securing or joining parts of a temporary outdoor structure—for example, an emergency overnight shelter.

TYING INSTRUCTIONS

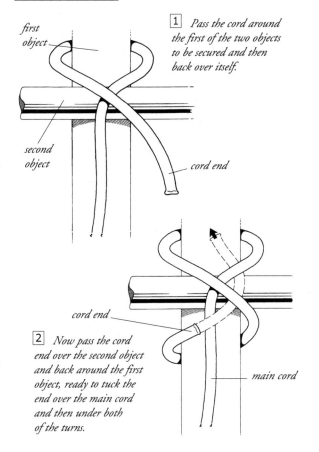

first object

second object

1 *Pass the cord around the first of the two objects to be secured and then back over itself.*

cord end

cord end

2 *Now pass the cord end over the second object and back around the first object, ready to tuck the end over the main cord and then under both of the turns.*

main cord

continued next page >

> *Transom Knot continued*

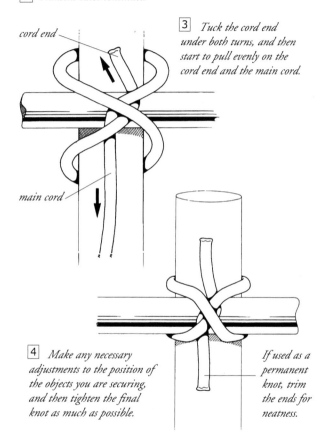

cord end

main cord

3 *Tuck the cord end under both turns, and then start to pull evenly on the cord end and the main cord.*

4 *Make any necessary adjustments to the position of the objects you are securing, and then tighten the final knot as much as possible.*

If used as a permanent knot, trim the ends for neatness.

>

BUILDING STRUCTURES WITH TRANSOM KNOTS

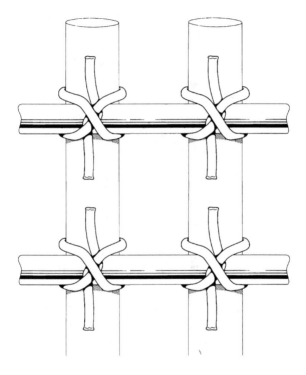

Correctly tied transom knots are very strong and will not slip, so an extremely strong structure can be built by joining together cross-pieces of various material with a series of transom knots.

TYING A NECKTIE—REGULAR KNOT

This may appear to be a simple knot, but how many times does the non–regular tie wearer suddenly find himself faced with a job interview or formal invitation and struggle to tie an acceptable knot? Probably over 80 percent of tie wearers use the regular necktie knot—or to give it its more precise name the four-in-hand knot. This knot is narrow and slightly asymmetrical. It is the perfect knot for a standard shirt.

NECKTIE FACTS

- Combine the fact that the necktie is the one element of a man's attire that has no obvious function and the continued predictions about the demise of the necktie and it is difficult to understand why sales of neckties are probably stronger now than they have ever been. World and business leaders are rarely seen not wearing a necktie, so presumably ambitious young leaders and executives will follow suit and ties will remain one of the keys to success.

>

TYING INSTRUCTIONS

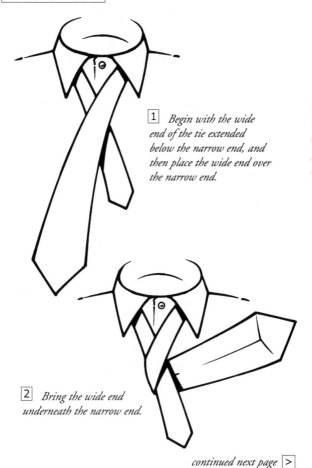

1 *Begin with the wide end of the tie extended below the narrow end, and then place the wide end over the narrow end.*

2 *Bring the wide end underneath the narrow end.*

continued next page >

> *Tying a Necktie—Regular Knot continued*

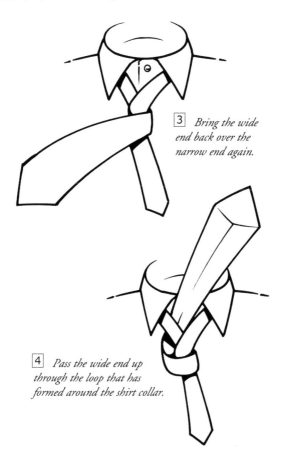

3 *Bring the wide end back over the narrow end again.*

4 *Pass the wide end up through the loop that has formed around the shirt collar.*

>

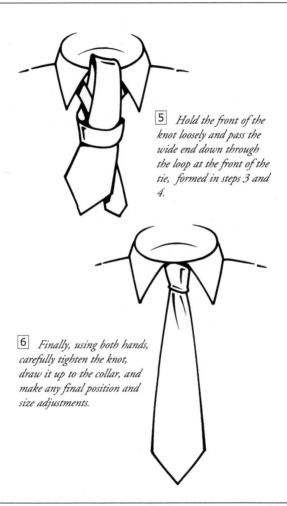

5 *Hold the front of the knot loosely and pass the wide end down through the loop at the front of the tie, formed in steps 3 and 4.*

6 *Finally, using both hands, carefully tighten the knot, draw it up to the collar, and make any final position and size adjustments.*

TYING A NECKTIE—WINDSOR KNOT

The slightly more complicated Windsor knot is a wide triangular knot that is ideal for wide collar openings. The knot illustrated here is the full or double Windsor and not to be confused with a half Windsor, which is a slight variation on the regular, or four-in-hand, necktie knot; see page 68. The Windsor knot is currently a very fashionable knot again and more suited to wide neckties and spread shirt collar styles; it may look crowded if you have a narrow collar opening.

NECKTIE FACTS

- The Windsor knot was popularized in the late 1930s by the Duke of Windsor (the former King Edward VIII). He was given credit for this stylish knot—hence its name—but it was almost certainly invented by someone else. This was a period of time when every well-dressed gentleman wore a necktie, so the knot caught on very quickly and was worn by millions of men all around the world.

TYING INSTRUCTIONS

1 *Begin in the same way as tying a regular necktie knot (see page 69) with the wide end of the tie extended below the narrow end, and then place the wide end over the narrow end. Now pass the wide end up through the loop that has formed around the shirt collar, then back down, and under the narrow end in the direction of the arrow shown in the step 1 illustration.*

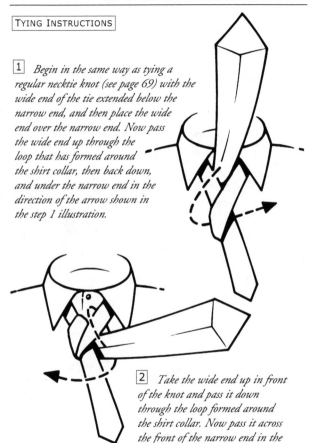

2 *Take the wide end up in front of the knot and pass it down through the loop formed around the shirt collar. Now pass it across the front of the narrow end in the direction of the arrow shown in the step 2 illustration.*

continued next page >

> *Tying a Necktie—Windsor Knot continued*

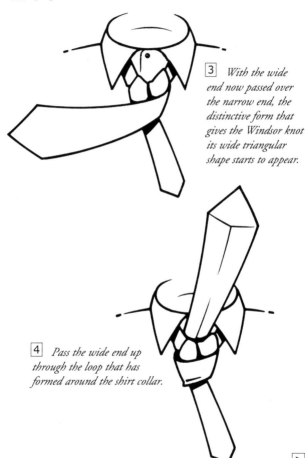

3 *With the wide end now passed over the narrow end, the distinctive form that gives the Windsor knot its wide triangular shape starts to appear.*

4 *Pass the wide end up through the loop that has formed around the shirt collar.*

>

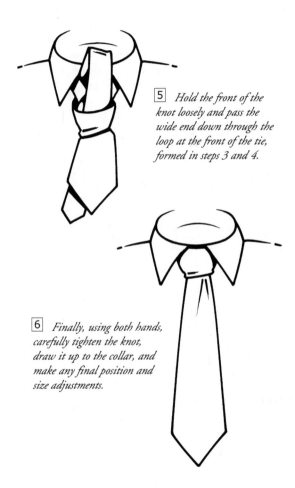

5 *Hold the front of the knot loosely and pass the wide end down through the loop at the front of the tie, formed in steps 3 and 4.*

6 *Finally, using both hands, carefully tighten the knot, draw it up to the collar, and make any final position and size adjustments.*

TYING A BOW TIE

The bow tie is the most classic of all ties, but tying it has always proved a problem for people who only wear one with a tuxedo for very special occasions such as a wedding or high school prom. In the past one of the complications of tying a bow tie has been tying it to the correct collar size. If a perfect bow knot has been achieved, it is all too often too tight, or too loose. This problem can now be easily eliminated by the use of

widely available adjustable-collar-size bow ties that enable you to set your collar size before you start tying.

BOW TIE FACTS

- The bow tie gets its name from the French *jabot* (pronounced *ja-bow*), a type of ready-made 17th-century lace cravat. By the mid-1800s tie makers started to shape bow ties to obtain definitive forms, including the form that is most popular and recognizable today. Black bow ties have become synonymous with formal and special-occasion wear and as the only proper complement to a tuxedo, but today with the explosion of bow tie colors and designs they are a fashionable alternative to the necktie.

> |

TYING INSTRUCTIONS

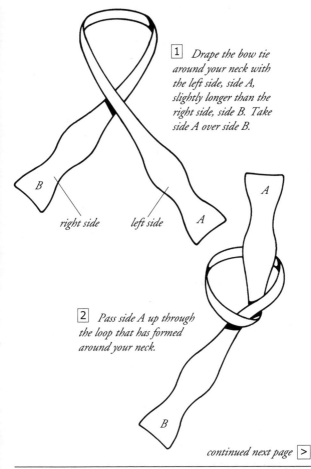

1 *Drape the bow tie around your neck with the left side, side A, slightly longer than the right side, side B. Take side A over side B.*

B

right side   left side   A

2 *Pass side A up through the loop that has formed around your neck.*

continued next page ▷

> *Tying a Bow Tie continued*

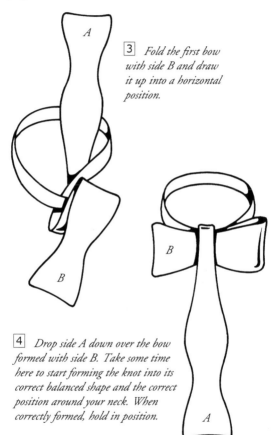

3 *Fold the first bow with side B and draw it up into a horizontal position.*

4 *Drop side A down over the bow formed with side B. Take some time here to start forming the knot into its correct balanced shape and the correct position around your neck. When correctly formed, hold in position.*

folded part of side A bow

5   Start to fold and position the second bow with side A. It is the folded part of this bow that will be pushed through to form the final bow.

6   Push the folded part of the second bow, side A, up and through the opening behind the first bow, side B, and in front of the original crossover on your neck. Make sure not to let the knot loosen at this stage.

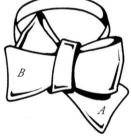

7   Continue to push the second bow, side A, through and into a horizontal position behind the first bow, side B. With the basic bow shape and center knot created, use both hands to pull, adjust, and tighten into the final bow tie.